MW00488743

Nail It

Stories for Designers on
Negotiating with Confidence

Ted Leonhardt
Seattle, USA

Nail It: Stories for Designers on Negotiating with Confidence
by Ted Leonhardt

Find us on the Web at: TedLeonhardt.com

To report errors or corrections, contact: errata@tedleonhardt.com

Author: Ted Leonhardt
Editor: Allison Laurel
Copyeditor: Jim Moore
Design: Allison Laurel
Illustrations: Ted Leonhardt

The information in this book is distributed on an "As is" basis without warranty. While every precaution has been taken in the preparation of the book, the author shall not have any liability to any person or entity with respect to any loss or damage caused or alleged to be caused directly or indirectly by the advice contained in this book.

ISBN 13: 978-0-9911727-1-9

This book is available at special discounts when purchased in bulk for premiums and sales promotions as well as for fund-raising or educational use. Special editions or book excerpts can also be created specification. For details, contact the author at the website above.

First printing January 2014

Belongs to:

Was lent to:

Acknowledgments

This book is for my wife and life partner Carolyn Leonhardt. Special thanks to Allison Laurel, editor and designer.

Thanks to the following for their help, advice and thoughtful comments along the way:

Larry Asher	Chris Laurel
Jean Culver	Anne Traver
Annabelle Gould	Len Stein

And thanks to all my clients and friends in the creative world who contributed their stories, thoughts and experiences to this book.

These are true stories, with some names and facts changed to protect the privacy of those involved.

Table of Contents

ted@tedleonhardt.com

About the Author

Seattle native Ted Leonhardt graduated from Burnley School of Professional Art and began his career as a designer. In 1985, with his wife Carolyn, he established the brand design agency The Leonhardt Group (now FITCH). Originating with a staff of ten, The Leonhardt Group grew to fifty employees and $10 million in annual fee sales by the time it was sold in 1999. Next, Ted served as Chief Creative Officer for FITCH Worldwide in London and held responsibility for 570 employees around the globe. He then served as president of Anthem Worldwide, a brand packaging design group.

Ted has lectured and written on the subjects of design and business for the University of Washington, the School of Visual Concepts, MakerHaus, the American Institute of Graphic Artists, the Association of Professional Design Firms, the Public Relations Society of America, and the National Investor Relations Institute. His writing has been published in *Marketing*, *Graphic Design USA*, *Communication Arts*, and *HOW Magazine*.

Ted is convinced that designers will play a definitive role in shaping the future. As an international consultant, he helps creative firms be better at what they do. He assists with financial dilemmas and people issues of all kinds, including partner disputes, acquisitions, team building, and difficult negotiations—his specialty.

Ted believes creative people have the power to improve the world, and that often they don't get paid what they deserve. His mission is to change that.

Introduction

Recently I was teaching a class on preparing for professional practice in the University of Washington Division of Design. I invited Ted Leonhardt to speak to the students on the subject of negotiation. The 90-minute class was a resounding hit with the students.

"I never knew that it was acceptable for a designer to ask for a certain salary without the employer saying something first."

It's hard to think of anyone more qualified than Ted Leonhardt to provide this advice. Ted brings to bear a lifetime of experience, from negotiating with employees, clients, and vendors to negotiating the successful sale of his company, and on to his current role counseling creative businesses.

"I've always worried about being too demanding when negotiating salaries."

I've known Ted since we were both fledgling design entrepreneurs. Ted's firm was widely respected for its excellent design work, but it also became clear that Ted brought a rare level of attention and focus to the business side of design. While so many designers have been driven by passion at the expense of business strategy, Ted has consistently demonstrated and spoken up for managing for business success.

*"I think now I will be confident in negotiating
a salary and making sure I portray myself as
being worth every penny I can negotiate for."*

These lively stories of negotiation dos and
don'ts provide more than a means to a better
paycheck. They illustrate a state of confidence that
empowers graduating designers and professionals
to step into the world as full participants: Speak up,
you are valuable, what you think matters.

*"Incredibly inspiring and useful. Ted taught us
how to walk in knowing your self-worth as a
designer and as a valuable employee. To never
work against the person negotiating with you, but
instead to sit, metaphorically, on the same side of
the table and work with them toward a common
goal: your getting employed by them."*

I was very pleased when Ted told me he was
preparing this book. Now his pragmatic view of
how to tackle these obstacles and grow from the
process will be widely available. Enjoy!

Anne Traver
Seattle, USA

Anne Traver is a design educator and an independent designer/
brand consultant. Named a 2007 Fellow by AIGA Seattle, Ms.
Traver was formerly co-owner of Methodologie, a brand design
firm founded in 1988.

The Stories

What was your first memorable accomplishment?

Stories that Teach

Wherever you are in your career, and no matter what kind of designer you are: If you want to freelance, work in-house, start your own boutique firm, contract internationally—or somewhere in between—you will benefit from this short compilation of stories you're about to read. I write to give you insights into how to handle difficult situations that can be a struggle the first few times you encounter them. With some background and practice we get better at it. I sure did. And so will you.

First let me begin with a story of my own, involving Niña, Pinta, and Santa Maria. To most, these names evoke the arrival of Europeans to the New World, but to me, they mark the first day of my career. This was the second grade. The moment when my teacher, Mrs. Hayes, called everyone's attention to the drawing I did of Columbus' ships was a big one. She praised the work and although

I was probably too shy to show it, I was proud, thrilled, and astonished all at the same time. I never forgot.

Turns out that big moment was the first of many. A pattern was forming, and it dogged me wherever I went. Even when I was made to repeat the fourth grade—a nightmare for me at the time— a traffic safety poster I created won a school-wide competition. The result? More walking on air.

This artistic ability was a really good thing, too, because I was a terrible student, and not involved with sports, school government, or much of anything else. My interpersonal skills were poor, my friends few, and my grades dismal.

The foundation of my career, my *life* even, was built on the ease with which I was able to create images that moved people. Those Spanish boats were proof: Design skills were all I needed to be recognized and successful. (Nod if this sounds familiar.)

As a young designer I advanced through several positions, always seeking a studio with fewer workplace complications. Eventually I had a dramatic compensation argument with an employer and left to start my own business. Looking back, I now realize that the money dispute was just one in a long line of unresolved issues. Yet even when I was running the show, I ran into the same predictable variety-pack of difficult situations.

These issues rarely changed. They were more like variations on a theme: clients who paid late; co-workers and vendors I couldn't reason with; a business partner I was powerless to confront when issues arose. Sticky fees, botched salary negotiations, ridiculous client demands, teams that didn't work well together . . . on and on.

The result was high staff turnover, diminished design quality, and an office that was on some days a bummer of a place to be. Through it all I was able to maintain the sales effort, so we didn't sink completely, but neither were we moving forward. We were just barely treading water. Clearly something had to give.

At this point my wife Carolyn and I were newly married with three sons, all of whom would be pursuing expensive university educations. So we dedicated ourselves to working on the business, not in the business. Carolyn is much more skilled interpersonally than I am, especially at seeing what is needed and speaking up about it. She focused on the internal people stuff, and I directed my efforts toward external relations. We hired a series of consultants, all of whom helped, even the one who recommended that I move back to design and let our VP of marketing take over. We fired him, but it was a wake-up call for me.

Here is the important part: Throughout this period I read piles of books about how to build a design business. I was seeking ways to turn our situation around. But I noticed that I had trouble translating the abstract business advice and studies into action. On the other hand, the career books that told stories and used examples to illustrate their points stuck with me. Connecting with their messages was a breeze. I easily recalled the stories and could apply their advice to my situation without much effort at all.

Using what I'd learned from stories, our firm finally started becoming prosperous, and we accumulated international clients and competitors alike. Now we were having fun. Developing our negotiating skills was undeniably important, so again: back to more books, training, and coaches. Again, the key to our learning, every time, was found in plotlines, anecdotes, scenarios, and firsthand accounts. Stories with a clear narrative thread were what we remembered, and we were able to put their lessons to work in advancing our success.

For millennia, humans have turned to stories to learn about life. No question, I'm a believer that our brains are hard-wired to think in terms of narrative. So it's no surprise that in addition to the pocket guide in your hands, most of my writing and blog posts use the storytelling format.

How did Karen score multiple job offers? Which one should she take? This is Theresa's first job; how can she possibly meet that insane deadline? Matt and Paolo absolutely need to agree to this client's terms. Or do they? As a designer, any kind of designer, even if you're just starting out, you're going to recognize yourself in these stories. You'll quickly learn what works, what to avoid, and how to devise your own plan by extrapolating from the true(ish) stories that follow. Most important, you will discover ways of getting comfortable with negotiating.

In the first section, I've assembled some favorite pieces that center on the dilemmas of job hunting

and salary negotiations. You'll meet the characters
Bridget, Ally, Andrew, Paolo, Carson, and Arianna
(among others), and hear details about their pre-
dicaments that you wouldn't otherwise have access
to. True to pocket-guide style, at the end of each
chapter I summarize my thoughts in a checklist
of what went well and what could have been done
better. Feel free to test my suggestions against your
own, then share the stories with colleagues or
mentors and see what they say. I invite you to get
engaged with this book. In so doing, you'll not
only have more fun, but you'll develop a comfort
level with these tricky topics that will be helpful in
the future.

This brings us to the second section, where I
deviate from storytelling and the topic of negotiating per se, in order to give some specific tips on
"acing the meeting." For example, did you know
you can stop an interview at any time and ask to
continue after a short break? This is a shocking
idea to most job seekers, even though once they
think about it, they see that it makes sense. Done
right, it could even earn you some respect. Hitting
the pause button is a move that's available to you—
but first, you need to learn how to use it.

Once you've become acquainted with negotiating and keeping your wits during a meeting,
we move to section three, where I offer business
development recommendations for the reader who
might want to start his/her own firm. For example,
in "Write Contracts, Not Proposals," I posit that
the best way to build a successful design practice is
by writing contracts instead of submitting

proposals. That's how my firm finally reached its potential. It's gutsy, but it's doable, and in the final chapter you'll learn how.

Being in control of your professional survival and creative happiness is an achievable goal. With the help of "Nail It," I hope you'll experience negotiating in a friendlier light, and that you'll feel confident about your ability to make positive things happen for you and the people around you. Let's begin!

What were you were paid in your previous position?

What am I Worth?

Recently I gave a talk to a group of design students on early career negotiations. Worth, and how to determine it, was very much on their minds. Three of the students shared their bargaining stories:

Margret
Focus: Publication Design
Region: Washington, DC

Laid off from her first position out of school (the company closed), Margret was interviewed at another company, where they offered her $45K. Then they asked her what her previous employer paid. She told them the truth and said $38K, so they lowered their offer to $40K.

The drop caught her completely by surprise. She went from feeling good to feeling sick and jilted in a heartbeat. Her self-worth had just dropped

$5K! The shock was physical; her chest clenched. What should she do?

My observations:

If she accepts the $40K, she'll lose their respect. If she asks for the original $45K, they'll attempt to get her down to $42K-$43K. If she asks for more, say $46K-$47K, they will be impressed with her confidence. She may not get the job, but she'll walk out with their respect—and her own.

What happened:

Shocked and dismayed, Margret turned down the $40K. The meeting ended. After a difficult wait, she's now expecting offers from two other employers. Above all, the experience helped her understand why she shouldn't reveal her past salary history, and to always ask for what she needs

Bridget
Focus: User Experience
Region: San Francisco

Shortly after graduation, Bridget was courted by some big firms in Seattle (where she attended design school) and eventually was offered slightly under $100K by two different firms in San Francisco. Naturally, these offers filled her with confidence. Better yet, one of them also offered Bridget an $18K signing bonus (although she favored the firm that had not offered the bonus). Both firms told her she couldn't tell competitors what she'd been offered.

Are her hands truly tied? Should she use the signing bonus offer as leverage?

My observations:

With little experience, Bridget needs all the advice she can get. She should turn to books, articles, friends, and/or family. Also, her cred is expanded significantly by the two offers. (Naturally employers use their power to hold down salaries.) Bridget should absolutely use the signing bonus as leverage to get the position she wants, and on terms she is happy with.

What happened:

Bridget told the company she favored that she wanted to work for them, but that she was concerned about the high cost of living in the area. She also told them that another company had offered her an $18K signing bonus. They matched it and she accepted.

Andrew
Focus: Brand Design
Region: Chicago

Andrew originally received two job offers. He told the first recruiter what his last position paid, and they offered him $2K more. Underwhelmed, Andrew declined. He then politely refused to tell a second recruiter what he'd been paid and was informed they couldn't make an offer if he didn't share his previous salary with them. The meeting ended. Andrew left with that sinking feeling you get when you suspect you pushed too hard. The next day they called and offered $20K more than he'd ever been paid. Why did that happen?

My observations:

Clearly, the recruiter was impressed by Andrew. The recruiter's offer, like all offers, needed to be based on an appreciation of Andrew, without the past salary as a reference point. Andrew raised the recruiter's respect by refusing to reveal his salary history.

What happened:

Andrew took the second position.

And, finally:

Widely available salary surveys provide a way for determining your worth, and it's important to know the range. Professional associations are the best place to start.

Still, developing the confidence to ask for what you need is an emotional skill, and harder to master than gathering pay-range facts. Learning to note and master your feelings during stressful situations is the real key to negotiation success, and with it you'll gain respect as well. This book and others like it can help (see Further Reading).

Ask yourself: Do I know what I need to succeed, and how to ask for it?

"I'd like to think about it overnight."

Karen Learns to Negotiate

On one of those blue-sky days when everything was going her way, Karen, who had just earned a degree in industrial design, landed an internship with a small firm that offered great work and a wonderful studio with a mountain view.

On their website was the kind of work that Karen had dreamed of doing for years. Better yet, they'd given her a three-month internship. It was unpaid (not the kind I recommend), and she knew she'd be doing grunt work, but it was an opportunity to work with real designers, for real clients.

The firm had fewer than twenty employees, but small was exactly what Karen wanted: a place where she could get to know everyone and learn how to be a professional industrial designer.

After a few days, Karen discovered that the firm's work had completely changed from what was showcased on their website. She felt let down, and a little bit tricked. Their current clients were in financial services and insurance, not the cool product design they had been doing for startups. She rationalized, "Oh well, it's only three months, and I'll learn something." So she stayed.

But then she became aware that the product development director was in a passive-aggressive war with the owner over the quality of the clients and the work. More seriously, the staff lined up in support of one leader or the other. Karen, being junior, uncomfortably found herself jumping from side to side just to survive. It was the longest three months of her life.

In the final week of her internship, with one of the firm's biggest projects completed, the owner fired the director plus six staff designers who had been at war with him.

Two days after that the owner offered Karen a full-time position at $25K a year. Their meeting felt weird, especially in light of the office drama and the owner's comment about his salary offer being "a lot of money for an inexperienced student." It made Karen feel like the offer was charity.

She felt deflated and insulted, especially since the offer was below her living expenses. Worst of all, she was so new to all this that she felt stressed, and the stress made it hard to think clearly. What to do? She restrained herself from reacting on the spot and said, "I'd like to think about it overnight."

Though her sleep was fitful, Karen did think about it overnight, plus she talked to her dad and a couple of friends, and got over feeling insulted. She didn't have any other opportunities, but her portfolio website was drawing increasing interest. So she decided to pass on the "charity offer" and start actively looking instead. Surely something would turn up.

The next day, Karen gave the owner her decision, politely saying, "The offer falls short of my expectations, so I have decided not to accept it." With that, she packed her things and left quickly. With a parting glance around the office she thought, "I will miss that view." It was her only regret.

The ensuing months were slow, and her funds dwindled. She picked up an engaging freelance assignment, but it wasn't enough to build a career on. Karen knew she wanted to be part of a group of experienced professionals, and that she needed the opportunity to compare her skills with others.

That fall, a retailer who was designing a line of small products interviewed Karen. The interview, with the head of the newly formed industrial design group, went very well. Karen was excited. "Cool products and a great group," she thought. "I'll be starting about the same time as everyone else, on the ground floor."

A month went by without a call. Karen had sent a thank-you, then emailed a follow-up note, but still nothing. "Perhaps the interview didn't go as well as I thought," she agonized. "Maybe I should have talked less, showed more work, asked more questions. Why do I always blow it?" In short, she was crestfallen and discouraged. Again.

But then, a different call and another interview, this time with a software company that had a large in-house industrial design group. They were creating devices for consumers and businesses. Feeling stronger (now that she had an additional opportunity), Karen called the retail director she'd interviewed with the month before. To her surprise he got right back to her. "Karen, sorry this has taken so long," he said. "I'd like to have you interview with a few other designers here next week."

The next two weeks were a blur of interviews with both companies. The software company offered her $50K to start. She mentioned the offer to the retailer and, amazingly, they offered her $52K.

Suddenly she had something to think about.

Karen proudly shared the news with her dad and best friends. The advice was the same from all of them: take time, be appreciative, ask as many questions as appropriate, think about what you want, think about which place feels best, think about which offers the best opportunity to grow.

Karen decided on the software company. She went ahead and mentioned the retailer's offer, not so much to get more money, but because she felt proud to be in demand. To her delight they offered her $54K. She took it.

I interviewed Karen after she'd been on the job for four months. She was learning quickly, loved her group, and was very happy and proud. And I was surprised to hear that she didn't feel that she had negotiated anything.

What can we learn from Karen's experience?

Keep your commitments. Even though three months may feel like an eternity, being known for keeping your bargains is important.

Think about any significant offer at least overnight. Take the time you need. Resist the urge to react immediately, even though the urge will be powerful. Resisting, in fact, makes you *more* powerful.

Expect your emotions to run wild. You're human, after all.

Always talk about major opportunities with people you trust. Their insights provide much needed perspective.

And, finally:

Sometimes negotiating is as simple as just mentioning your other opportunities. It's a less confrontational way of asking for what you need.

Intense interest is a huge advantage.

Chuck Zeroes In

Upon earning his hard-earned bachelor's degree in marketing, Chuck decided to take time off to be a snowboarding instructor. He taught in the winter and mountain-biked all summer. Teaching was fun and gave him incredible people skills, but Chuck couldn't deny his growing fascination with design, spurred by the remarkable snow journals and websites all around him. He returned to school, this time for an associate's degree in graphic design with a Web focus. After graduation, he gathered background on the firm whose creative director had presented about recent findings in cognitive research to his UI/UX class. Chuck found the subject thrilling, and when he learned that the creative director was a former skateboarder, he knew he'd found his firm.

To prepare, Chuck studied the firm's site, downloaded their book, read and reread it. He did

the usual Google and LinkedIn searches, followed
the creative director on Twitter, and studied the
sites and interfaces the firm created. Then, through
a manager at the firm who was one of Chuck's
repeat snowboarding students, he landed an invite
to a party in their offices celebrating a recent
product launch.

Chuck located their building in a redeveloped
light manufacturing area near the bay. The office
had grand floor-to-ceiling steel windows on the
north side, where Chuck found the guests chatting.

Chuck had prepared a series of questions, but
asked just one: "How are your competitors re-
sponding?" The client whose product was being
launched turned toward Chuck and answered in
some detail. Later, one of the senior developers
complimented Chuck on his question and asked
about his background. Chuck communicated
his interest in the firm and asked if they had
any openings.

The conversation led to an interview and a
freelance UI assignment. The work was tough, but
that didn't matter—Chuck was freelancing for his
dream firm and mountain-biking. He was in heaven.

Right after Thanksgiving, the practice leader
told Chuck that budget was available to offer him a
full-time position starting the first of the year. Over
Christmas he shared the great news with his family
and asked how to negotiate the next steps. He was
particularly concerned about time off, as he still
loved the outdoors.

Chuck's mom pointed out that his hourly freelance pay ($50) was likely higher than what they'd

offer in salary. She said, "Your freelance rates were high because the firm did not provide health care, vacations, or other benefits." Mom also noted that freelancers command higher rates because they risk periods of unemployment.

"Pay rates often become an issue when a firm hires a former freelancer," she continued. "Management is trapped by the existing salary structure, so they have to offer substantially less on an hourly basis. Also, Chuck, forget about the time off for mountain-biking and snowboarding. They'll expect you to be on the job every day."

Chuck hadn't thought of that. He was just doing the work and enjoying himself, but he still loved the firm and wanted that full-time position.

His older sister had recently negotiated her salary with a large consulting firm. Her advice was to think of the $40K he'd been paid so far as a baseline and to mention the annualized $100K as a friendly but throwaway request. "Mentioning one hundred sets the top of the range," she explained, "with the bottom being forty. It lets the other party know that you know your value, but are reasonable." She thought Chuck should ask for $80K but be willing to accept $60K, which would leave a good margin for the firm.

Chuck's appointment with the practice leader was on January 3. He arrived early thinking, "I shouldn't have had the second cup of coffee. I'm probably too alert." Sally, the practice leader, smiled and said, "Chuck, I'm so happy that we can offer you this position."

"Thanks, Sally, I'm really looking forward to being here full time."

Then he went ahead: "Sally, I did the math and discovered that if I stayed busy as a freelancer I'd make a hundred thousand this year." Then he paused, feeling anxiety sweep over him. His neck suddenly felt prickly and he hoped that he wasn't blushing.

Sally's smile disappeared. "You know, Chuck, freelance rates are much higher than the salaries we pay…"

Chuck interrupted, remembering that his sister had said to establish his anchor before Sally had a chance to state a number, "Sally, I understand, so I thought eighty thousand would be appropriate." He paused, feeling better. Sally didn't seem angry; everything seemed okay.

"Chuck, your work has been terrific, but we have pay scales based on job categories, and I can't pay you higher than others. It wouldn't be fair." Chuck remained silent, as his sis had instructed.

Sally went on, still friendly but in a more serious tone, "Chuck we're able to pay you seventy thousand plus a full benefits package with health care and two weeks of vacation after a year."

Chuck thought to himself, "Wow, ten grand higher than expected, but a year without vacation? I can't do that." So he said, "You mean I can't take vacation for a year?" "Not paid vacation," Sally replied.

Chuck pulled out his iPhone and did the math, "That's fourteen hundred a week. Could I take unpaid vacation?" "I guess you could; that would be up your team members and the demands of the project."

That felt better. He wanted the job. He wanted to say yes, but sis had been insistent: "No matter what they offer, think about it overnight." So he thanked Sally warmly and asked her permission to think about it.

The next day Chuck called Sally, said yes enthusiastically and confirmed the details.

What can we learn from Chuck's experience?

Being intensely interested gave Chuck a true advantage. So let your feelings show if you fall in love with an opportunity, because genuine attention is extremely appealing.

Thoughtful questions demonstrate commitment. Write down what you'd like to ask beforehand.

Freelancing often leads to a well-paid position, because it allows the client to see the candidate's skills in action and allows the candidate to see if the position feels right.

The party that throws out the first number establishes the range. In Chuck's case, he effectively moved the range up by starting high.

Chuck was nervous, but he had a plan. That gave him a sense of control over the outcome and helped him feel better. Clear, easy-to-remember plans are a proven way to relieve anxiety.

Chuck used his advisors successfully. In effect they acted as his negotiating team, and while they were not in the room with him on the big day, he would say that he could feel their presence.

And, finally:

Chuck was not only passionate about this opportunity, he had also put the effort in. It shows once again how hard work plus effort pays off.

Ask those hard questions when you think of them.

Carson Becomes a Professional

After graduating with a degree in graphic design, Carson's college placement office set up three job interviews for him: a position in a PR firm's in-house design group; an art director position with a local ad agency; and a combination design and illustration position at a small design boutique.

Carson met with the ad agency and the PR group, but it was the design boutique that caught his imagination. He felt immediately that it was the place for him. He chuckled as he recalled the creative director's almost single-minded pursuit of creative awards. "Awards, acclaim... I'll be famous too," he envisioned. "What a great place."

After a second interview with the owner, the boutique group offered Carson a position at $26 an hour. He quickly did the math and discovered to his delight that it worked out to over $50K a year. This was riches for Carson, who had been making

$25K–$30K a year waiting tables while going to school. Carson felt somehow more alive, he was so happy.

Once his buzz wore off, Carson realized that they had only signed him up for three months. They'd sort of passed over that point quickly during the discussion. This realization gave him a moment of discomfort, but after reflection it seemed fair—they didn't know him, after all. He thought, "Well, I'll work hard and do the kind of award-winning design they want, and I'll be in long-term."

He didn't bring up the subject of the three-month trial on the first day. He just wanted to get to work and show what he could do. And he sort of didn't want to say anything that would spoil the good feelings.

The three months passed in a blur of happiness. Those first months were thrilling. Carson supported the creative director with the design and illustration work he loved to do, plus he got to work directly with clients and even supervised the work of the freelance illustrators the agency used. However, Carson did notice that the agency paid the freelancers the same $26 an hour he was getting.

When the three months were up, the owner called Carson into her office, and with a big smile said, "Carson, we love you and your work. You've been doing a great job; frankly, you've exceeded all our expectations. We'd like to offer you full-time employment."

Carson thought, "Great, she's going to offer me a raise!" Then she said, "Your starting salary will be twenty-eight thousand a year."

To Carson, it seemed like all the air had rushed out of the room. "What?" he exclaimed, "Twenty-eight thousand? That's half what I'm making now. That's less than I was making waiting tables. You said my work was great."

"But, Carson, that was our freelance rate," she countered. "We've been paying you as a freelancer— no benefits, no vacation, and no insurance. Now you'll have all that, and you've got a full-time position. The twenty-eight thousand is for a full-time position. It's more secure than freelance."

He was stunned. Or maybe crushed would be a better word. "Maybe," he told himself, "I'm not as good as I thought." He swallowed hard and worked to keep his game face. He wanted this uncomfortable moment to be over.

He didn't want to leave the firm and start all over again looking for a new job. He could actually make more money waiting tables. After all, he'd made $30K working part-time. But the boss had been a jerk, Carson remembered, hitting on the women and cheating on the tips whenever he could. And he loved it at the firm! The work was great, the people terrific... though now it didn't feel quite as good.

He very briefly thought about going freelance. A quarter of his classmates were freelancing, and some of them weren't doing too badly. But that would cut him off from coworkers, and he liked the feedback he got from client connections. Additionally, the little boutique was well positioned with California's housing industry, a fact Carson loved. The clients were the biggest homebuilders and developers in the state, and they were all booming. The work was fun, the clients great to work with, and the budgets seemed unlimited.

Carson felt hooked. He asked to be reviewed every three months with the potential for a raise if he did well, and accepted the offer.

He stayed three years, learned a ton, and gradually had his salary raised to $38K. Eventually one of the clients had moved to a large wine and spirits marketing company, and he recruited Carson to fill a $50K position in their brand design and promotions group. When he gave notice the creative director told Carson that even she wasn't making $50K. She also said she deeply regretted losing Carson.

Today, Carson runs his own design consultancy and routinely produces six-figure branding programs, a far cry from the $28K he started with.

What can we learn from Carson's experience?

Carson's drive and desire to get started kept him from seeing that he was being hired as a freelancer.

Had he managed his emotions better, he could have asked more questions in his early interviews, and that would have prepared him for dealing with the freelance-to-salary issue.

When he was in that awful meeting, feeling startled and worried, he could have excused himself and taken a walk. Or even asked to reschedule the meeting for another day after he'd organized his thoughts and gotten his emotions under control.

He could have explored staying freelance—
there was more than enough business, and they
were keeping several freelancers busy.

He could have asked for a couple thousand
dollars more salary when they offered him the
$28K. Or he could have requested more vacation.

And, finally:

It's important to note that, for all its imperfec-
tions, Carson took the job that made him happy.
The fact that it was a modest start didn't prevent
the opportunity from developing into a very
rewarding career.

Understand the issues and the underlying interests.

Ally Lands a Brand

J ust nine months after graduation, Ally got her first opportunity to design a brand program. It was through a connection she'd made with Tom, a creative director at the city's largest design firm. She'd shown him her book several times, and he'd retained her to provide alternative designs for a large client. He liked her approach and thought of her for this new assignment, which his firm was too busy to take on without assistance.

Ally had only eight weeks to create and produce the visuals. She knew from a friend who already worked there that if the firm did the work, the fee would be $150K. Ally calculated that working on the project full-time for eight weeks at $150 per hour, her fee would be $42K, maybe even $60K with the extra effort.

Tom didn't ask Ally for a budget. He just sent her the files with a note: "Get going, and remember, you'll need to present at 10:30 a.m. January 30. Oh, please check in with me in a week."

(Projects occasionally get started without a formalized contact or advance payment. Why? Because everyone is in a hurry to get going. People are mostly trusting of others, but it is good to check around on the firm you'll be working with. Check in with your network, including instructors, peers, and other freelancers.)

Ally thought, "No budget required? This is dangerous. I'll get started, but I'm also going to send a budget." Reasoning that she'd need some help on the project, Ally called Beth, one of her former classmates, and engaged her at $30 an hour.

Ally calculated, "Sixty thousand plus, say, ten for Beth—that makes it a seventy-thousand-dollar project. That leaves the agency room for margin. They'll be able to double my fees." It sounds like she was throwing a lot of numbers around for a new designer, but Ally was from one of those families that lived and breathed business. In fact, her billing insights came directly from an uncle who'd worked in the design industry for years. So she sent her budget to Tom, and just to be safe, she copied Anne, the account manager.

Over the next week Ally's studio felt like it had graduated to the majors, with sketches and roughs pinned to all the walls. She and Beth were totally into it. At week's end she gathered up their thinking and bused down to show Tom their work. He loved it.

When Tom had completed his review, Ally asked him if he'd had a chance to approve her budget. He said, "Oh, that's right; Anne wanted to talk with you. Could you stick around for a few?" And off he went searching for Anne.

"She's in meetings, but she'll call into this conference room in a minute." They stepped into the room just as the phone rang. Tom answered, "Hi Anne, Ally is here with me."

Anne responded, "Hi. Sorry I had to rush out, but with all these product launches I'm always on the run. We're launching on four continents and in fifty countries just now. Ally, we love your work and know that you're just perfect for this new brand. But our client is in severe belt-tightening mode, so I must inform you of the terms our client requires. We'll write you a check for five grand today; I know you'll need it for expenses. We'll cut a check for the balance ninety days after you've completed work."

Ninety days? Ally couldn't wait ninety days. She needed that money. Her stomach flipped like a roller coaster, her knees felt weak, and her vision narrowed. Then she remembered something her uncle had said: "Ally, never negotiate when your emotions have control over you." He also said, "Take the time you need. You have all the time in the world; there is always more time than you think. And remember, don't ever be defensive."

Back to the call: Ally said, "Anne, this is too important to talk about on the phone. Could we talk in person? What's your time like Monday?" Anne agreed to meet.

Shaken, Ally called her uncle and arranged to grab lunch. After she told him her story he said,

"Ally, the tight schedule gives you leverage. They must have your work on the 30th for that presentation. It's too late for them to get anyone else, and they know it. I'd assume Anne has some problems with billings on the account, and that she thought that you, as a kid, would just roll over.

"On Monday, Ally, start by asking her to help you understand why such a fine firm and such a great client would have such a slow pay policy. Then wait for her to respond.

"Then change the subject to other issues. Ask follow-up questions about the client, their branding programs or market position. Aren't they growing and gaining a significant market share? Why are they launching this new product now? Have there been significant market changes affecting the company? Have there been management changes?

"Get Anne to talk as much as possible. Listen for the issues that could have led to her demands. You want her to see you as someone who is interested in the big picture, as someone she needs to keep happy because of your ability to contribute to her success.

"No matter what she says, she will be more agreeable and more comfortable after she's had a chance to talk about the account and the issues, in person."

Ally spent the weekend memorizing her talking points and felt prepared when she walked into the meeting with Anne on Monday. They talked for more than an hour, and uncovered a series of issues Ally could help with. The breakthrough moment came when Ally suggested that they go together to meet with the client's marketing team and show them the preliminary designs. They did, and the meeting went well.

After that client meeting Ally raised the question of payment. Before she could even state her case, Anne said, "Don't worry about it, Ally. Bill us for half now and half at the end of the project, and I'll see that you get paid quickly. I can find other places to save."

What can we learn from Ally's situation?

Ally wisely didn't attempt to defend her position; instead, she asked for clarification. When people are defensive, they reveal themselves as feeling threatened and vulnerable. Far better to focus on solving the client's situation.

She developed a relationship with Anne by joining with her in uncovering the issues.

She took the time she needed to gather her thoughts and respond.

She used her advisor.

She changed the context from payment to helping the client.

Ally was clearly focused on helping Anne and her client. She put them first without needing to give up anything.

She didn't let Anne's condescending manner frighten her.

And, finally:

Remember, the tight schedule gave Ally the leverage she needed.

Have you gone from euphoria to fear in an instant?

Matt Gets an Email

Despite its status as a fledgling startup, Matt's group won a major project even though they had been pitted against two gigantic management consultancies and a global branding agency. Even better, they won on their unique set of skills—not price.

Matt's group had already been working a couple weeks. The project was off and running without a contract, which gave them major leverage. Along with his art director, Matt was asked to present to the client weekly; they had just finished their first presentation. In this meeting, they clearly demonstrated their mastery of the assignment. Everyone in the room felt it: They had shown impressive progress. And then this email arrived:

Hi Matt,
My name is Judy Smith and I'm with Alpha
Group's procurement department. I work

with Larry and the Charge-It team on their contracts. I've taken a look at your fees for the brand/product design. They're just a bit higher than we usually pay, so I'm wondering if we can discuss how to lower these rates a bit.

Also, we notice your firm is billing the same amount ($195 per hr.) for a principal and senior associate. Normally we've found a senior associate rate to be lower than the principal rate. I'm hoping we can discuss this too.

Email or phone is just fine—I'm mostly available today and Wednesday if that works for you.

Thanks!

Judy Smith J.D., LL.M.
Senior Contracts Administrator
Global Innovation Team
Alpha Group

The color drained from Matt's face. Recovering a bit, he thought, "What's this? We're already doing this job! Are we going to get paid? We've just put in two intense weeks of work. What happened?"

After asking Paolo, his senior associate, what he thought, Matt picked up the phone and called his client in order to tell her about the email and ask for help understanding it. She sounded very uncomfortable, even a bit evasive: "Matt, you'll have to deal directly with Judy on this."

Matt persisted, saying, "But we have the assignment, right? The team seemed in agreement that we were on track and making good progress. We've been working with you for two weeks. Do you know Judy Smith? Why is a lawyer involved? Don't we have a deal?"

"Just call Judy, Matt. I'm afraid I simply can't get involved."

Two weeks in, and purchasing has reared its ugly head. That's never a good sign. Matt's mind was spinning. What now? Call Judy Smith, that's what. Then his intuition spoke to him: "No, don't call her. Send an email, and set up a time to meet." So he penned:

> *Hi Judy,*
> *Just read your note. Paolo and I will be in your offices all day tomorrow. Could we get a few minutes to meet to discuss your concerns?*
> *Matt*

He hit Send, hoping for the best. Then he printed out Judy's original email to study, and made a few notes:

- Seems like artificially friendly language.

- Judy is a procurement lawyer assigned to the Charge-It team.

- Not just a lawyer, but a lawyer with an advanced degree: LL.M.

- She seems to be comparing our fees to others, but who?

- The comparison of principal to senior associate is clear. How to handle this?

- Seems like she's looking for any angle she can get.

- Email/phone is not fine. We must meet in person.

- Her title is senior—not VP or SVP, just senior— some power but not total power.

Organizing his thoughts helped Matt feel better. He talked it over with Paolo, and they decided they would take the following approach:

- Tell Judy that we only discuss fee issues in person, not over the phone or by email.

- Meet with her together, so she'll see that we are qualified professionals.

- Explain that Paolo leads the product design team, and Matt leads the branding team. The difference between us is that I'm an owner and he's not, but there is no difference in the value we bring to the project.

- Explain that we set fees based on feedback from our clients. We're fully engaged on this project, so we take that to mean our fees are acceptable.

- We know our competitors charge two to three hundred dollars an hour. At $195 per hour we're a bargain.

- We've found that when a consultancy lowers its fees, word gets around, respect suffers, and so does the project.

- Finally, we've found that results matter, not the fee.

Matt and Paolo felt good about their position. Better yet, Judy replied quickly, setting up a meeting the following afternoon. "Come to eighth floor reception and my assistant will get you," she wrote.

They arrived on time, took a seat, and proceeded to wait forty minutes. When they were ushered into Judy's office, she was sitting in a tall chair with her back to the windows, the bright afternoon sun blinding their eyes.

Feeling confident, Matt thought, "First the wait, now this—it's just another trick." Yet an urgent thought also raced through his mind: "Why the games?"

Instinct told him he had to ask for what he needed. "Judy, could you lower the blinds, or could we move to another room? We can't see you." They quietly relocated to a different room, and then things moved quickly. They talked, and she asked again for lower fees. Matt and Paolo politely declined. With little more to say, she thanked them for their time, and the meeting wrapped up. A signed purchase order to cover the project in full was sent the following week.

So what was this all about? They had the job, which meant she had no leverage. They learned later that Alpha Group's policy is to always ask consultants to lower their fees. And about twenty percent of the time they get the fees lowered. It's important to be prepared for this kind of maneuver, especially when dealing with large organizations. Of course, anytime the purchasing department is involved, you have to brace yourself.

This behavior isn't meant to be personal. It's just business. But when what you're selling is personal—as thoughtfully prepared design tends to be—there's no question that it feels personal. Very personal. So don't let that throw you. Take a deep breath and stick to your position. It will get easier in time.

And, finally:

Always be aware of your leverage and the advantage it provides. Don't let the pressures of the moment distract you.

Vulnerability is closer to the surface for creatives.

It's Not Business; It's Personal

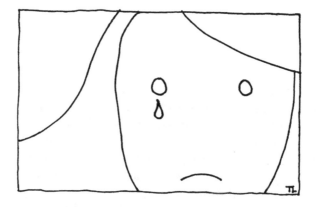

After graduating with a degree in interior design, Arianna took a municipal position helping the mayor envision possibilities for the city's iconic central train station. The six-month project resulted in a keynote presentation and print document that Arianna created. The entire project played to her strengths, as she had both graphic and interior design skills. Additionally, her role was well defined, so she was okay with the leadership expected of her.

No question—the train station project was a great launch for her career. The mayor gave her an award of excellence for her leadership on the project, and local interior design professionals celebrated her effort online.

Flush with optimism from this initial success, Arianna moved across the country to interview with large architectural firms that had in-house interior design groups. It was late 2008, and although her recent acclaim had paved the way to several encouraging interviews, no positions materialized. 2008 was not a typical year; after all, most firms had suffered significant layoffs. It seemed the only opportunities were freelance or contract.

After weeks of fruitless searching, Arianna was offered a contract position: no health care, no vacation, and no benefits. Worse, it was for just one month. She was actually considering taking it when her dad said, "Taking a gig like that would be like throwing yourself under the bus!" He was thinking about all the years and expense—school, internships, laptops, and training—that she'd invested to get, what, a month's contract? "Unacceptable. Absolutely unacceptable," he said.

"But Dad, I'm almost out of money. At the very least this will connect me to people actually working in the field."

Arianna's dad was a highly sought-after physicist. He worked in the medical field designing ultrasound machines, and his services had always been in demand. In fact, his reputation was so well established that he never even had to seek work. His advice to Arianna had always been, "Be humble, be a top-notch performer, defer to authority, and they'll come to appreciate you." Once, he'd even boasted that he'd "never had to negotiate a fee." And that was true. Early on it was all about grants, but even when he transitioned to corporate clients they always paid whatever he requested. Negotiation is demeaning, was his stance: "Just do good work, and you'll be fine."

Arianna thought, "Sure, but he hasn't had to

scrape for an entry-level job during a recession. Isn't this different?"

Just as Arianna was about to accept the one-month contract, a three-month offer from a larger firm with a stand-alone interior design group fell in her lap. She took it instantly.

Arianna immersed herself in the work and the team soon recognized that her combination of graphic abilities, interior design skills, and mastery of the software was a real asset. Arianna found herself building presentation after presentation that showcased the team's thinking. Even though she didn't always think the firm's solutions were as strong as they could be, as a temporary contractor she kept her doubts to herself and focused on making the work look the best she could.

Throughout these early weeks Arianna plugged away on her own, often working through lunch and into the evenings. She had always been quiet and introspective; long-term friendships were what sustained her. But here, all the way across the country from where she'd grown up and gone to school, she was feeling lonely.

When the three months were up, her supervisor, Mary, called her in for a review. "Arianna, your work has been great, and we'd like to extend the contract for a couple more months," Mary said. "We're in a big push for new business, and we need your fine hand on the presentations the partners are requesting. However, there is one thing that has been a disappointment: We need you to be more involved. Previous staffers always gave their opinions and would point out where the designs needed improvement."

Arianna was taken aback as Mary went on. "In those reviews, when we're all gathered around the plans, you never say anything. Why, Arianna? Your work is terrific. I'm sure you could contribute something. Okay?" She continued, "Actually, I just heard that I have the budget to hire a designer for the interiors team. Are you interested in full-time status?" Arianna's heart leapt. Until now she had been depressed over the feedback, but here was a real job. "Yes, I'd love that!"

"Great," Mary replied distractedly. "Thanks, Arianna, I need to dash to a meeting..."

Arianna walked out of the office on cloud nine, completely forgetting the "You don't speak up enough" comment in the review.

With new motivation to impress, Arianna redoubled her efforts, working late, skipping lunch, and keeping her nose to the grindstone.

A few weeks later, one of her team members called her attention to a job posted on the firm's site. It described Arianna's position perfectly. Apparently it had been posted for a while, because fifteen candidates had already submitted applications.

The next day a new designer was introduced to the group and Mary dropped by Arianna's desk to introduce him.

"Brant, Arianna is on contract here as a specialist. There are two more weeks in her contract." Turning to Arianna, Mary said, "Could you spend some time filling in Brant on our requirements before you go? That would be a big help. Thanks, Arianna."

In a daze, Arianna excused herself and made a beeline for the restroom. She was heartbroken, completely taken by surprise, and crying her eyes out. After a few minutes another woman in the group came in and gave her a hug. "Don't worry, Arianna, I heard about another firm that's hiring, and I know someone there. I can't believe how horrible Mary was. We all thought you were perfect for the job, and we were just as shocked as you when the listing went up on the site." In truth, her teammate had communicated doubt to Mary about Arianna's ability to collaborate, but she was eager to make Arianna feel better (and relieve her own guilt while she was at it).

Arianna recovered over the weekend, then trained Brant, who was not a bad guy. She finished out the contract and toughed out a trying five weeks before being hired by the other architecture firm (for more money than she was earning at the first one, as luck would have it). She was thriving at the new firm, but when Arianna shared this story two full years later, it was still so painful that tears came to her eyes.

What can we learn from Arianna's experience?

Success takes more than keeping your head down and doing the work you've been assigned. In creative settings, a collaborative nature is expected.

Ask what is important to your supervisor when you accept a position. Any position. In her haste to say yes, Arianna made the common but erroneous assumption that a contractor is not a "real" member of the team.

Resist the urge to be a lone wolf. Personal interactions are key to creating a bond with one's group. Without them, chances are low that anyone will advocate on your behalf.

Still waters run deep? Not in most creative departments. If you don't speak up, your team will think you have nothing to say.

Sometimes one's family and life experience can shape actions the wrong way. Even a successful person who cares about you might be in the dark when it comes to the nuances of your situation. Arianna was right to use her own judgment.

When you receive challenging personal feedback, take time to talk about it. Find out what it means. Ask for suggestions. Understand what you can do to change. (If a supervisor doesn't assist in your efforts to improve? Simply put, it isn't a good workplace. Start looking for a new position.)

Resilience is immensely helpful. Because Arianna bounced back quickly, she was able to pursue what turned out to be a better job than the one she was leaving.

And, finally:

Emotional pain stays with us, often for life. We always remember when people make us feel bad. Remember that when you have power over others.

Acing the Meeting

Will you recognize this one as a loaded question?

They'll Ask; Don't Tell

If you're asked what you were paid in the past—and most interviewers will ask—your answer will determine whether you will (a) be fairly compensated for what you're worth, or (b) walk away from income that should be yours.

Wondering how one might sidestep this inevitable question? Here are some things to say that will shift the focus away from old salaries to your current worth:

Turn it around with a question

"What are your expectations for this position? I'd like to get a feeling for what you're looking for."

Let them know that you hold their interests in high regard

"I'd like to find a job that's a good fit for me and my next employer. I expect to be paid current market rates for my skills and experience—to be paid fairly for what I contribute."

Position the interviewer as the expert with the knowledge

"I assume you have a budget and a fair idea of what this position is worth to your company."

Emphasize that past pay isn't relevant

"What I've been paid in past positions is not relevant to my current value or future performance. I've added valuable skills and experience since then."

The it's-none-of-your-business answer

"My past compensation is a private matter between me and my last employer. It would be a violation of that trust to reveal it."

And finally, just say no

"No, I won't do that."

I know this feels awkward. It may even feel inappropriate. You naturally feel like you need to accommodate the interviewer. You think you have to be compliant and obedient, and you feel extremely eager to please. But all those feelings work against you. You will appear to be much more valuable, and more powerful, if you politely refuse to answer this loaded question. If you do tell, the interviewer will peg the new offer to your past compensation, and you'll leave money—and more important, respect—on the table.

Confrontation avoided. Problem solved?

Never Lie About Your Past

When you're negotiating, sometimes it feels like it would be so easy to tell a little lie to advance your position, or to avoid an uncomfortable confrontation.

There you are at the bargaining table, and you're asked what your salary was at your previous position. You know it's a really bad idea to tell. You know that if you do tell, your chance of getting a significantly higher number will be greatly reduced. You know that you're supposed to politely explain that it's none of their business. But in that instant you think it would be so much easier to just add a few thousand dollars and tell them a number. Confrontation avoided. Problem solved.

You think to yourself: "It's just a little fib. In the scheme of things it's nothing. They'll never find out. No one will ever know. And I'm really worth that number anyway."

Don't do it.

We all know lying is wrong, but at a weak moment when we feel vulnerable it can seem like the easy way out. And who doesn't feel vulnerable when their self-worth is being negotiated? But here's the thing: When you lie you miss the opportunity to demonstrate your real value—the value of your character. Your power, self-confidence, and the opportunity to show that you believe in yourself are too valuable to risk. Because above all, prospective clients and employers want to work with people who are capable and confident—people who are comfortable in the way they conduct themselves in the world. Asking for what you need is a demonstration of those traits.

So, uncomfortable as it may seem, politely saying no to their request actually raises your value in their eyes.

People lie all the time on résumés and in employment interviews. They add degrees not completed and universities not attended. They list positions not held and responsibilities they weren't responsible for. It costs them directly when they are discovered, and it takes a personal toll even if they're not discovered.

Never forget that if you do lie and exaggerate your past compensation, your employer may find out later. The revelation will ruin the relationship—it's unlikely to be forgotten or forgiven.

Finally, if you're anything like me you'll constantly worry about it. It may not keep you awake at night but that lie will reside in that special corner of your mind, where the unresolved issues dwell for a very long time. Also, fibs and exaggerations are notoriously hard to keep track of. The chances that you could accidentally contradict yourself in the future are high.

Go ahead and draw a line in the sand. Ask for what you need. Base your compensation request on your credentials and accomplishments. Never lie about your past.

Get what you need to be successful
for them and yourself.

Twelve Tips for
Negotiating Your First Salary

Negotiating your first salary presents a major challenge. You have not been trained in the art of negotiation. You face strong competition, have a deep emotional connection to your work, and often feel some insecurity about your talents.

The following tips are designed to help you get what you need.

TIP 1: PLAN

Negotiation produces anxiety, and anxiety is caused by unknowns. Negotiation has lots of unknowns: Will they offer me a job? How much salary should I ask for? Is my work up to their level? Will they like me? Luckily, planning diminishes uncertainty. Make a list of the unknowns and knowns. The more items you can move from the unknown to the known side of the paper, the better you'll feel. Even just the process of making lists and planning will reduce your anxiety and prepare you. Professionals never negotiate without a plan.

TIP 2: KNOW THE RANGE

Every negotiation that involves money has some kind of a range. Salary, consulting, and free-lance ranges are published regularly by professional associations. These third-party sources provide credibility for the amount you request, and they're updated annually. Just knowing the range should reduce your anxiety considerably.

TIP 3: ASK FOR THE TOP OF THE RANGE

Get your salary request out first. Research has shown that the first number mentioned establishes the range in the context of the discussion. If you ask for the top of the range, or a little more, it's more likely you'll get a higher salary or fee. Assume that your negotiating opponent knows the range. If they pretend to be shocked, cite your sources. Just getting your request out on the table should help reduce your anxiety.

TIP 4: DO NOT ACCEPT THE INITIAL OFFER

If they do state the salary or fee first, assume there is more money available. In business, some attempt to negotiate is expected. It's expected that the initial amount will be challenged. The initial offer is never the real budget; if you don't ask for more, they'll lose some of the respect they initially had for you. This applies to all settings—in-house and staffing agencies too!

I've always believed it's up to me to show others my value to them. It's my job to let people know how I can help them. (Or not.) My skills, and yours, are not right for all, but they are exactly right for some. So I enter every final negotiation with the assumption that the other party wants to hire me, and that I'm there to confirm that feeling.

TIP 5: SHOW RESPECT

Be respectful, and expect respect in return. I was once asked why I wanted so much money, and I answered with, "Respect. Respect for my skills and experience. If you don't respect me, I won't be able to help you." It is entirely appropriate to have a high, but realistic, opinion of yourself and your accomplishments. Remember, you've spent your whole life preparing for this moment. Asking for what you need shows that you respect yourself, and that you expect respect in return. Those who ask for what they need get respected. (It took me years to learn this one and to act on it. I hope you'll be able to use it much earlier in your career than I did!)

TIP 6: STUDY THE FIRM—BE INFORMED

Study their website, LinkedIn info, Twitter feeds, and Facebook. Do a news search. Ask friends, family, and any connections you have in common about them. Know why they're hiring. Have a general understanding of what they're looking for, and the issues they seem to be facing.

TIP 7: LISTEN MORE, NARRATE LESS

Use your research to prepare a few relevant questions. Remember that asking is much more powerful than telling.

Listening is a powerful tool. Listen, take notes, read back what you wrote, and ask for clarification. You'll learn what they're really looking for and how it will shape the interviewer's personal future as well as that of the company. The more you learn about the firm and the more informed you become, the more comfortable you'll be negotiating with them.

Ask them why they're interested in you. When they answer you'll know more about what your value is in their eyes. When follow-up questions come to mind, ask them.

This is a good time to point out that being really listened to is immensely flattering and engaging. You'll learn more about the opportunity—but you'll also build a personal bond with the interviewer if you're an excellent listener. Here are some examples of what you might ask:

- Why have you created this position?

- Why this project at this time?

- What are the company's goals? What are your goals?

- What effect will it have on the company, division, yourself, the world?

- How do you envision moving forward?

- What effect will it have on the market? On competitors?

- Who will I report to, and why?

- Who will we need to get approvals from? And why?

- Who will be on your project team?

- What are competitors doing that will impact our efforts?

- What's the model for success? For failure?

- Have you undertaken anything like this in the past? What was your experience?

- How is this effort viewed in other departments within the corporation?

- Are there groups that will be advanced by the project?

- Are there groups that will feel threatened?

Remember to always hold back one question that you can use at the end of the interview when you're asked, "Do you have any further questions for me?"

TIP 8: AVOID TALKING TOO MUCH

Talking too much is a sign of discomfort and neediness, which a trained negotiator can exploit. Don't do it. Your prepared questions should help you avoid this trap.

TIP 9: DON'T GIVE THEM ANYTHING FOR FREE

If you don't value your work, they won't value it either. Always get something in return for everything you provide to the client. In the market economy we live in, everything that is of value is measured in money. If you don't ask for a fee for what you provide, the client will not value it.

TIP 10: NEVER RUSH TO CLOSE

Recognize that negotiating is the first step in a creative process. Take all the time you need to understand every step, every detail of the process. Be guided by the phrase, "I have all the time in the world." Rushing to close is another classic sign of weakness and insecurity. You must guard against this feeling. Often we're so uncomfortable negotiating that we race through the bargaining so we can get to the work. No surprise there; doing the work is our first love. But don't let that derail getting paid what you deserve.

TIP 11: NEVER REVEAL YOUR PAST SALARIES OR FEES

We're all needy. We all want others to know that we're valued. Often, in a misguided attempt to prove that we're valued, we reveal too much. Feeling compelled to tell what we were paid in the past is an example of trying to prove our worth.

Don't do it. Past compensation is a private matter between you and those who paid you. If asked directly what you were paid, just respond that you can't say because it's a private matter. If that doesn't feel right, revisit the other options in "They'll Ask; Don't Tell."

Rest assured that interviewers will use it against you if you do tell. Worse, they'll feel taken advantage of if they're paying significantly more than what you'd earned in the past. They'll ask; don't tell. It's that simple.

TIP 12: GET AS MUCH AS YOU CAN

I know it sounds harsh. But that's what negotiating is all about: getting what you need to be successful for them.

I don't believe in "win-win" negotiating, because it sets you up to give away too much right from the outset. Most people don't really study how win-win negotiations are practiced and written about by the pros. People commonly think it's as simple as giving up something first, so the other party will see that you're a nice and reasonable person. But that's achieving a different goal.

Of course your goal of getting as much as you can is balanced with your need to create and maintain a successful long-term relationship (everything rests on that beneficial relationship) but don't enter with the mindset that you're going to give things away that matter to you.

Getting recognition for yourself
and your work. **Or not.**

Restart, Leave, Get Control

Presenting yourself as a creative professional comes with a special kind of pressure. You're representing not only yourself, but yourself plus the work you've done. Not only are your appearance and performance examined, but things you create with your hands, heart, and mind are judged as well.

This aspect of being a creative professional comes with a heady combination of highs and lows. The excitement of the creative process brings with it a big dose of worry about how our work will be received. We creatives undoubtedly get into this business because of the thrill of doing the work and getting recognized for it.

The truth is, I've seen people come to tears in these highly charged meetings. I have a clear memory of a former firefighter who, in his first professional interview with me for a creative assignment, broke into tears. He cried because he was deeply emotionally attached to the work. The memory of an adult man crying over his work will be with me always.

Sometimes during a stressful interview or negotiation, we feel overwhelmed. These meetings are important; they're critical to our future. In extreme circumstances you may find your vision narrowing, notice a pounding in your ears, feel a cold sweat, or experience any number of other sensations. These "out of balance" feelings can happen to anyone.

Or you might find yourself with nothing to say, and that's bad enough. (It's happened to me.)

When forcing yourself to continue the meeting—trying to suppress the feelings—it's likely that the discomfort will return. Simply "getting past it" doesn't work. At least in my experience it never did.

What does work is taking direct action. The easiest action is to take a break from the discussion, saying something like: "I'll just take a moment to think about this." Politely rise from your chair and leave the room. Say, "I'll be back in a minute." Don't allow your opposite to stop you.

Or you could say, "I need just a moment to compose myself." This just might get the interviewer to rethink his or her approach.

Of course you can always say, "Could we pause for a few minutes? I'd like a break."

Be aware in advance that you can excuse yourself. It's important, because when you're in the room and feeling pressed, you must recognize that these anxious feelings are a signal to take action. If you're not aware of this option and prepared to take it, the anxiety could take over and reduce your ability to deal with the situation—or worse, cause a breakdown like the firefighter's.

To do your best for yourself and your client or potential employer, you must be at your best. In fact, taking a break honors the importance of the meeting. You're doing it in the spirit of doing your best!

Once you're heading for the restroom, you'll feel much better. The simple fact that you took action to regain control will make you feel better. With your confidence returning, think of a couple questions to use once you're back at the table. Questions are another method of maintaining your confidence. Questions will help you gain more control of the situation and demonstrate your interest. Taking the break gives you a chance to restart and regain control of the encounter.

Returning to the meeting, you need to restart the conversation:

- You could say, "I was surprised to hear you say _____ . Could you explain further?"

- You can enlist the interviewer's help in getting past the situation with: "Is there a way we can work together to solve this?"

- Or one of my all-time favorite questions: "Help me understand why _____ creates difficulty for you?"

- Or: "Let's try to think of ways to meet both of our needs."

All these questions use neutral language and are used, obviously, in a spirit of mutuality. You're showing your desire to collaborate. All are in the best interest of you and your negotiation opponent. Best of all, they put you back in control. With control you'll feel stronger, better, and worthy of the consideration the hiring firm is giving you.

(Ah, yes, the firefighter did get the assignment, but it took a second meeting to seal the deal.)

Winning and Keeping
New Business

Wondering how to get their respect?

Respect, PowerPoint and the C-Suite

When a client, prospect, or potential employer asks you for something, or to do something, you have their respect. After all, they wouldn't be asking if they didn't respect your ability to fulfill their request. In that moment you have their attention. Their request provides you with the power to ask for something in return.

You may think asking is risky. You may think that asking could lose you the opportunity. You may think that asking will disrupt the good feelings going on in the discussion. But your thinking would be wrong.

It would be wrong because asking for what you need at that moment, at that very instant, demands respect. If what you ask for is clearly in their best interest, and requested in a manner that is direct, clear, and completely neutral, you'll increase their respect.

One of my client's young designers, Polly, was assembling PowerPoint presentations on site for a group of C-suite* executives for a Fortune 500 client. The day of the big show was rapidly approaching, and tension was running high. The work was consuming; a typical day started early and often ended after midnight.

The demanding schedule had gone on for a week. Polly was exhausted and almost at her wits' end when she finished up the last of the changes for the CTO's presentation with his assistant, Theresa, early Sunday morning. Theresa was new, just six weeks into the position, and was clearly afraid of what would happen if she let Robert down. He had gone through several assistants and had a reputation for being demanding.

At 1 a.m. Theresa emailed the completed show to Robert and said, "Thank god, that's it for now. You can go get some sleep, Polly; thanks for sticking with me on this."

This was Polly's second year of working on this show, and she'd had similar experiences with these C-suite executives in the past. So she asked Theresa, "When is Robert's rehearsal scheduled? Is it on Tuesday when the others are?"

"Yes, he's set for 10 on Tuesday."

"That means we'll only have Monday to make any changes," Polly noted, "and I'll be jammed most of Monday revising the rest of the decks."

"Well," Theresa responded, "Robert will be traveling with the tech team all day Monday. I don't think he'll have much time to work on this."

97

"Then you need to call him tomorrow morning and ask him to closely review the deck. We need to get his changes as early on Monday as possible. He has to look good for the rest of the team at Tuesday morning's rehearsal," Polly replied.

"I can't call him tomorrow. It's a Sunday! Sunday morning. That's totally rude. He'll go nuts on me. He told me he's expecting me to handle this."

Then Polly said, in a calming voice, "I know what he said. He always says that. But Theresa, he'll respect you more if you just carefully explain what's at stake here. He wants to look good. He wants to perform well on Tuesday just like the others. I know you've done your best in assembling this deck, and, in fact, it looks and sounds just right to me. But I also know that he'll want changes. They always do. It's impossible for you to know exactly what's in his head or what he wants to say. So your call is in his best interest. Why not frame it as a thoughtful heads-up that will help him prepare for a demanding week?"

Theresa began to feel better about calling Robert. "It is a once-a-year event, and he does need to be at his best," she said. "I'll call him at 10 a.m. Thanks for pressing me on this, Polly, I think you're right."

"Call me after you've talked, Theresa," Polly replied. "I'd like to hear how it went."

By modeling for Theresa how to make a request in a direct, clear, and neutral manner, Polly felt like she'd made a friend and a significant contribution to the effort, too. Additionally, she felt valued not just for her design skills, but for her contribution to the overall success of the event.

* C-Suite refers to the senior executives of an organization. They're the decision-makers, and their job titles typically begin with "chief," as in Chief Executive Officer, which is where the "C" comes from.

A loaded situation.

It's Not About Money

B ob is a successful principal and oversees a group of fifteen architects within a large multidisciplinary design firm.

He called the other day and said, "I'm hiring designers for new positions, and also doing salary reviews. How do I explain our pay scale? I use the AIA Compensation Survey as a guide, but I always feel uncomfortable talking about money."

Join the club! Everyone is uncomfortable negotiating salary. It's so personal, putting a hard measurement on our performance. All creatives are anxious about measuring up to expectations—their own and those of others. Creative managers are just as sensitive to these expectations, so salary meetings are loaded with highly personal impressions.

You'll become more confident in those conversations as you become accustomed to their interpersonal dynamics. The professional surveys are great for establishing salary guidelines, so use them as a point of explanation along with your budget and employees' performance. You'll find that people will accept salaries that are within those ranges if everything else feels right to them.

PRIORITIES BEYOND PAY

When creative people want higher salaries than the surveys indicate or budget allows, it often means that something besides money is amiss. Most studies find that money is the third priority for people who work in creative services.

The first priority is what we could call the "belonging factor." Designers want to work in a cool place, with others whose work they respect and for leaders they believe in. They want to be part of a team that is doing great work for interesting clients. In short, they want to belong.

The second priority is the "contribution factor." They want others to respect their work and value their contribution. They want to know that their individual efforts are regarded as significant additions to the team. They want to work hard, and to have fun as part of a group that includes them.

Money comes third. Everyone wants to be paid at a level appropriate for his or her skills, experience, and contribution. But creatives are mainly motivated by the work itself, and the status the group achieves through it.

The opportunity to do great work as part of a respected group makes people happy. In turn, happy people make money for the firm and for themselves.

BUSY CREATIVES ARE HAPPIER CREATIVES

Creative shops are happy places when there's slightly more work to do than is required. (Calculate how many hours to expect from a billable employee—35 hours per week × 50 weeks—to determine revenue targets and workload.) Then focus your sales effort on achieving five to ten percent more than that.

Creative people like to be busy. Therefore, the worst thing for a studio is to not have enough to do. It's demoralizing, and it can destroy budgets as people expand their project workload to fill their time. Happiness is a delicate balance between being busy and being overwhelmed.

VISION CLARITY AND UNRESOLVED ISSUES

Here's another way to look at it: First your firm must have a clear vision of where it's going and why it's a good idea to go there. There must be a purpose that everyone understands and believes in. Second, that purpose must be demonstrated every day in the interpersonal dealings between people.

Issues arise all the time between people in groups. But for the firm and your group to thrive, they must be resolved. Major damage occurs when interpersonal issues are left unresolved. Unresolved issues and lack of a well-understood vision are the two most common problems I encounter in my consulting.

People feel good when the direction of the firm matches their personal beliefs and values. When issues are dealt with directly and swiftly, it reinforces the feeling that "I'm a part of a good team." It demonstrates that the firm is committed to a future they can count on, a future they can trust.

Ultimately, the key to happy people is doing great work to the highest standards, and maintaining a group that respects the contributions of all its members. It makes us happy when others want what we have to offer. And clarity on where we're going and why it's right to go there makes salary negotiations much easier.

Do you know how to generate
a continuous supply of work?

Tell Your Story and Create a Virtuous Cycle

2 | Develop insights and stories

E very freelancer's question: How to get work? And, more important, how to create a continuous supply of work with acceptable fees? How about continuous work at more than acceptable fees?

STEP 1: DO THE WORK

A virtuous cycle is a series of events that results in a favorable outcome, time and again. For creative professionals, it means using your work and the insights gained from your experience to attract the attention of future clients. The first step in the virtuous cycle is doing the work. Remember, the work you do and the perspective you bring to the each project is what differentiates you from your competitors. You are unique—therefore your work is unique.

STEP 2: DEVELOP INSIGHTS AND STORIES

Each creative project adds to your personal knowledge base, and this includes school and pro bono projects. This knowledge base provides the opportunity to form insights that will help future clients succeed while furthering your differentiation from other design firms. Those insights can form the base for stories that share your perspective with prospective clients. Remember, these stories must be about how your work helped your client succeed. (Or, if it was a school project, how your unique approach helped the design succeed.) The stories are about you only as reflected by your design's, and your client's, success.

STEP 3: GET YOUR STORIES IN FRONT OF PROSPECTS

Email campaigns, public speaking, article placement, new business pitches: These are all places to tell your stories. Your site, your blog, LinkedIn, Facebook, and print and online publications are all valuable for placement. These are not case studies; case studies commoditize. You don't ever want to turn your talent into something that is evaluated on price the way a commodity is; there's far more to your services than what they cost. Your stories must be personal; they must be heartfelt narratives about helping others to succeed. Tell them with understanding and humility.

STEP 4: RESPOND TO INQUIRIES

Inbound calls are proof that your virtuous cycle is working. They mean that the caller accepts you as an expert, at least to the extent that they want to know if you can help them. They have read a story, seen you speak, or been referred to you, and what they know about you aligns with a need they have. That inbound call means that as an expert, your fees become "non-negotiable." (Remember, if you do respond to pressure to reduce fees you'll lose some of your power in the relationship.)

STEP 5: BEHAVE LIKE AN EXPERT

It's important at all times to behave like an expert. Throughout this process you must maintain and advance your expert status. One easy shortcut to behaving like an expert is to memorize and use the phrase "In my experience…" as often as possible. Even as a student, simply saying "In my experience" subtly and persuasively reminds the listener that you're acquainted with this situation, and that you have an awareness and education to draw from. What could be more "expert" than that? Other examples of expert behavior are characterized by:

- Proactively determining how to best meet client needs.

- Asking questions and creating plans.

- Developing lists of deliverables required to achieve success.

- Developing budgets required to accomplish the scope of work.

- Writing contracts, not proposals (more on this in the next chapter).

Why the virtuous cycle is important:

Learning to think of your work as only the first step in the process of gaining influence and opportunity is critical to achieving success.

No matter whether you work for yourself or for someone else, the five steps of the virtuous cycle will attract the opportunities that fit you and you alone, thereby furthering your unique expert status.

Obviously, you'll have a much more satisfying career if your talent is in demand.

A well-managed virtuous cycle, combined with real expertise, erases the need to negotiate.

I've written this book to help you, but please note: It's just a continuation of my own virtuous cycle.

You've spent your whole life
preparing for this moment.

Write Contracts, Not Proposals

Did you know that it's possible to skip the proposal? Well, it is. When a prospect responds positively to your virtuous cycle and decides to contact you, you'll be in position to tell them how you can help them. And in so doing you'll be summarizing what could be a proposal, but by doing it verbally you can skip the written proposal entirely and just follow up with a contract.

The key to staying in charge of the transaction through this step is in how you present your approach and summarize what needs to be done, how long it will take, and what it will cost.

Prospects want you to be knowledgeable, powerful, and in charge. They expect you to tell them how you'll help them. You must start by listening to what they need. Next, ask as many questions as possible. Make sure it's clear that your questions are in the spirit of helping them. Then summarize what you've heard and ask for corrections or feedback. Finally—and this is the important part—describe how you will help, addressing these three critical points:

1. What will fill their need?

2. How long will it take?

3. What will it cost?

The next step is to ask if they agree. If not, listen carefully to their response and correct your approach as needed until you're comfortable you've gotten the three points right.

You've now arrived at your final step: **Follow up with a contract.**

This is how to close deals that really help your clients get the full benefit of your insights and expertise. This is also the way to close deals with better-than-acceptable fees. When you're in charge, even if you are new to the industry they want you to know what it will take to solve the problem (including the fees).

Whether you are a junior designer or a creative director, remember that you've spent your whole life learning and preparing for this moment. You're educated. You have skills. You follow industry journals and attend design talks. You know who to turn to with questions. And you know that you chose this career in order to help others. Be confident in using the experience you have.

"I wish I'd said…"

A Final Word on Emotions

Feeling hindered in the moment is universal. There's a French saying, *"Avoir l'esprit de l'escalier,"* which means "to have the spirit of the staircase." This refers to that familiar experience of thinking of what you wanted to say on the stairs (or in the elevator) after having left a conversation. It's about being tongue-tied at the exact moment an intelligent response was needed.

I've learned over a long period of time how to manage emotions and stay present when negotiating. By now, I do what I do instinctively and automatically. That can make for a teacher who can't explain how to do what he does, because in essence he no longer knows how he does it. So to balance that, I tell stories that make it possible for you to practice being in tricky situations yourself.

Still, there are a few tactics to follow when dealing with the emotions that accompany difficult conversations:

- Keep a list of your accomplishments in your pocket.

- Review your credentials before a big meeting, such as degrees earned, notable positions held, workshops attended. Even achievements such as taking the blue ribbon in a cooking competition or finally beating your sister at chess are legitimate and have value.

- Practice what you want to say beforehand.

- Spend time imagining a positive outcome to the meeting; set the expectation in your mind that things will go well.

- Be prepared. Do your homework. Know as much as possible about the situation and who you're dealing with.

- Take a quick walk beforehand, get some fresh air.

- Remember that humans are social first. The other people in the room are having their own emotional responses, too.

- Take your time. Breathe. There is no rush.

Further Reading

Difficult Conversations: How to Discuss What Matters Most
by Douglas Stone, Bruce Patton, Sheila Heen, and Roger Fisher

The Dyslexic Advantage: Unlocking the Hidden Potential of the Dyslexic Brain
by Brocke L. Eide and Fernette F. Eide

Graphic Artists Guild Handbook: Pricing & Ethical Guidelines, 14th Edition
by Graphic Artists Guild

Women Don't Ask: The High Cost of Avoiding Negotiation—and Positive Strategies for Change
by Linda Babcock and Sarah Laschever

Notes

Notes

Notes